W9-AAP-980

WORDLESS
WORKSHOP

WORDLESS
WORKSHOP
BY ROY DOTY

Reader's Digest

THE READER'S DIGEST ASSOCIATION, INC.
Pleasantville, New York/Montreal

Copyright ©1996 The Reader's Digest Association, Inc.
Copyright ©1996 The Reader's Digest Association (Canada) Ltd.
Copyright ©1996 The Reader's Digest Association Far East Ltd.
Philippine Copyright 1996 Reader's Digest Association Far East Ltd.

All rights reserved. Unauthorized reproduction, in any manner, is prohibited.

Library of Congress Cataloging in Publication Data
Doty, Roy, 1922–
        The family handyman Wordless workshop/Roy Doty.
            p.   cm.
        A collection of wordless cartoons entitled the Wordless workshop
published in the Family handyman magazine.
        Includes index.
        ISBN 0-89577-875-0
        1. Woodwork—Pictorial works.   2. Storage in the home—Pictorial
works. I. Doty, Roy, 1922– Wordless workshop.
II. Family handyman.   III. Title.
TT185.D5797   1996
684'.08'0222—dc20   96-2747

Reader's Digest and the Pegasus logo are registered trademarks of
The Reader's Digest Association, Inc.
The Family Handyman is a registered trademark of RD Publications, Inc.
Printed in the United States of America.

Dear Reader:

Over the years we've received a lot of mail from readers of *The Family Handyman* magazine about Roy Doty's "Wordless Workshop." Most of their letters, postcards, and notes are short—very short, actually. Much more concise and to the point than the usual reader letters we get that tend to go on and on about something they thought we should have done better in the magazine, or something that's broken in their home and they want our advice and help and assistance *right away.*

Fans of "Wordless Workshop" keep it short and sweet. They write, "I like your magazine a lot. I like Wordless Workshop the best." That's it! It's as if the power of Wordless has left them...wordless!

Hmmm. All the work we put into words and photos, and editing and designing long, complicated articles...and a huge number of folks choose the all-cartoon-no-words-one-page "Wordless Workshop" as their favorite!

Such a powerful idea in so small a space. A committee could not have done it, that's for sure! Roy Doty deserves the credit for creating it and keeping it going so successfully.

Enjoy the book. I hope it leaves you **speechless.**

Gary Havens

Gary Havens, Editor

Dear Reader:

I have had a lot of fun drawing the **"Wordless Workshop"** over the years. As an amateur handyman and non-technical illustrator, I created the cartoon strip as a way to explain do-it-yourself projects in a simple, humorous style. In the cartoons Mr. and Mrs. Workshop, as I think of them, set up the problem, and the step-by-step art that follows tells the story. No words or measurements get in the way.

I began the strip 40 years ago, inventing the projects myself. Soon "Wordless" readers (the strip appeared first in *Popular Science* and in the last five years in *The Family Handyman*) joined in, dreaming up and submitting simple projects that make life easier or better. For years they have been sending photos, making stick drawings, and writing letters describing their ideas. Readers are loyal, and "Wordless" has become something of a family tradition: the "Boot Cleaner" project (pp. 142–43), for example, was submitted by the grandson of an original "Wordless" reader.

The recent projects featured here are among my favorites. I hope you enjoy them as much as I enjoyed drawing them.

CONTENTS

CABINETS,
CLOSETS, AND SHELVES

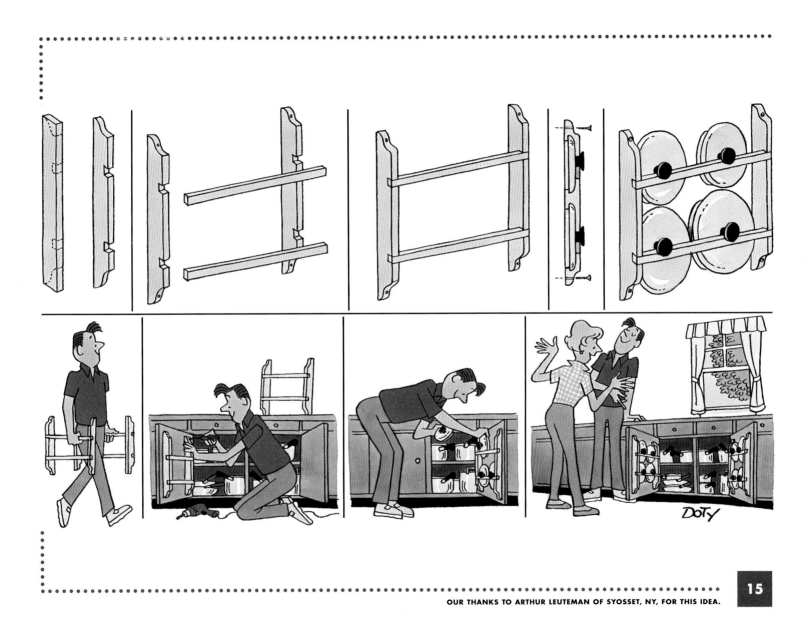

OUR THANKS TO ARTHUR LEUTEMAN OF SYOSSET, NY, FOR THIS IDEA.

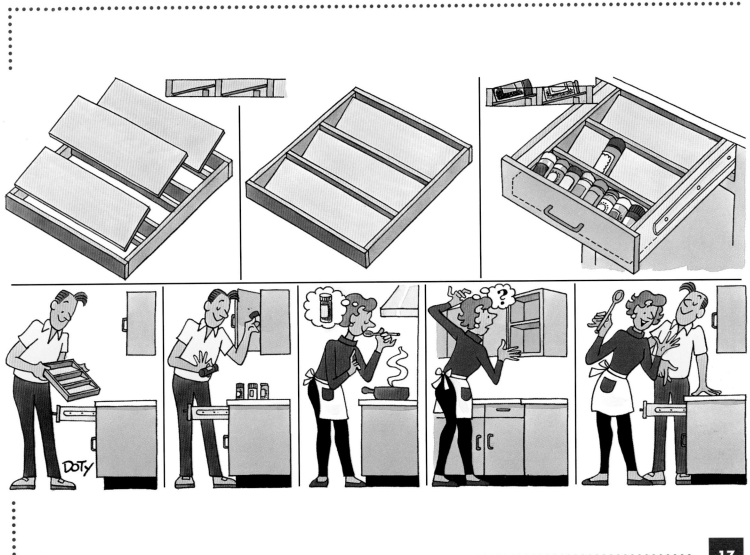

OUR THANKS TO HENRIK LAGERQUIST OF PITTSBURGH, PA, FOR THIS IDEA.

OUR THANKS TO TIMOTHY STREM OF BAKERSFIELD, CA, FOR THIS IDEA.

OUR THANKS TO FRAN PAUL OF COLLINGSWOOD, NJ, FOR THIS IDEA.

OUR THANKS TO JOANN AND STEVE GRIFFITH OF MARIETTA, GA, FOR THIS IDEA.

OUR THANKS TO GERALD R. SNYDER OF AMSTERDAM, NY, FOR THIS IDEA.

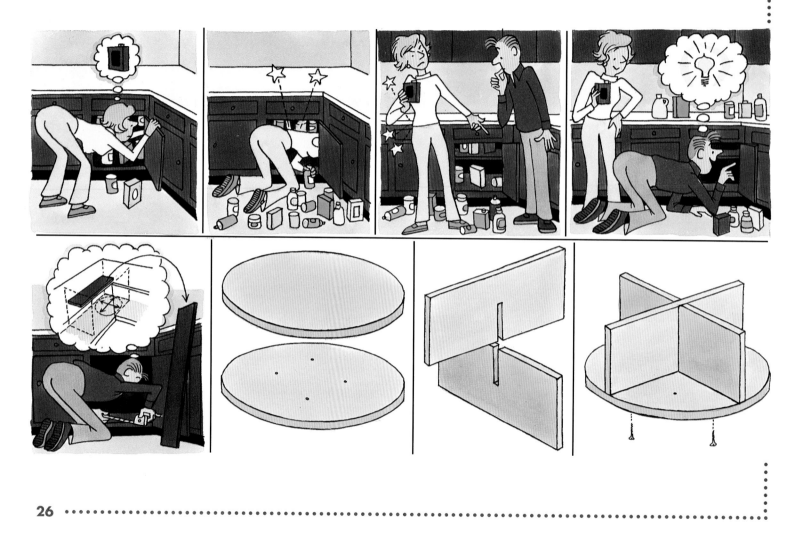

OUR THANKS TO ADA DUBAY OF MINNEAPOLIS, MN, FOR THIS IDEA.

OUR THANKS TO JUANITA RHAME OF HOLLY HILL, SC, FOR THIS IDEA.

OUR THANKS TO MAX GLASHEEN OF RIVERSIDE, CA, FOR THIS IDEA.

OUR THANKS TO HENRY A. CIARALDI OF OCALA, FL, FOR THIS IDEA.

AROUND THE
HOUSE

OUR THANKS TO LINDA CUNNINGHAM OF BROOKFIELD, WI, FOR THIS IDEA.

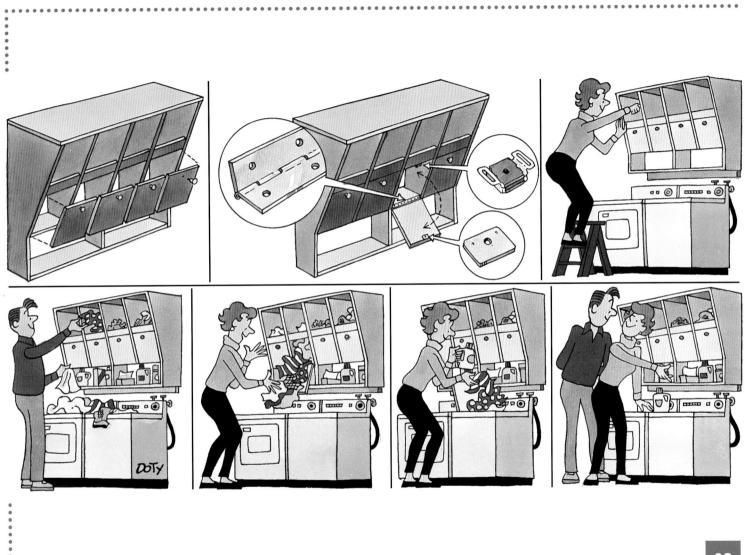

OUR THANKS TO LARRY JOHANSON OF CHANDLER, AZ, FOR THIS IDEA.

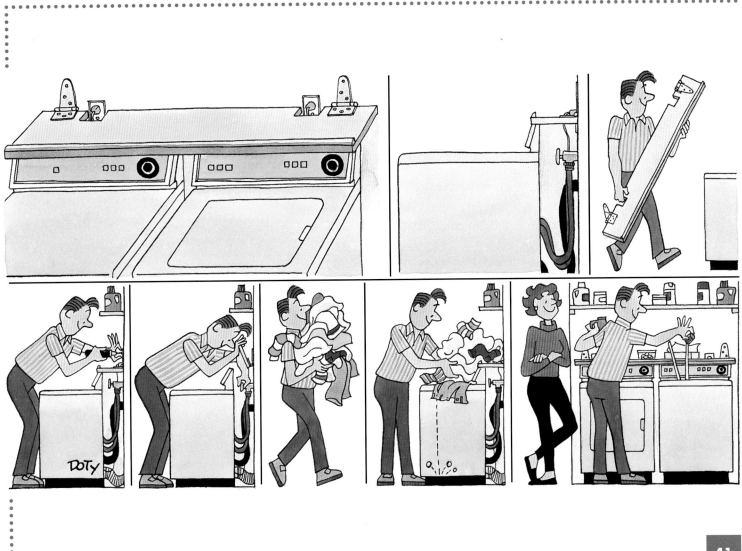

OUR THANKS TO JOHN ESKRIDGE OF KILLEEN, TX, FOR THIS IDEA.

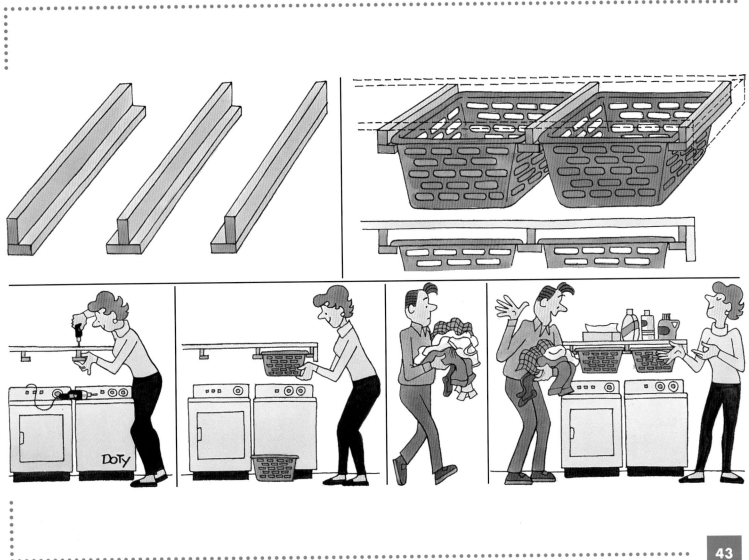

OUR THANKS TO AL BUGGERT OF MESA, AZ, FOR THIS IDEA.

OUR THANKS TO WALTER F. REGEHR, JR. OF AUSTIN, TX, FOR THIS IDEA.

OUR THANKS TO BYRON KIRBY OF ANTIOCH, TN, FOR THIS IDEA.

OUR THANKS TO JOHN HENDRICKS OF FRASER, CO, FOR THIS IDEA.

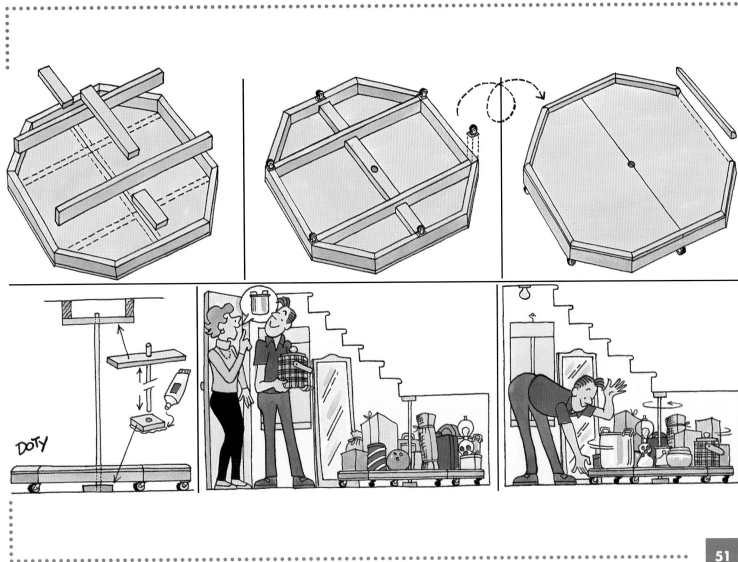

DOTY

OUR THANKS TO STEVE SINCLAIR OF EDEN PRAIRIE, MN, FOR THIS IDEA.

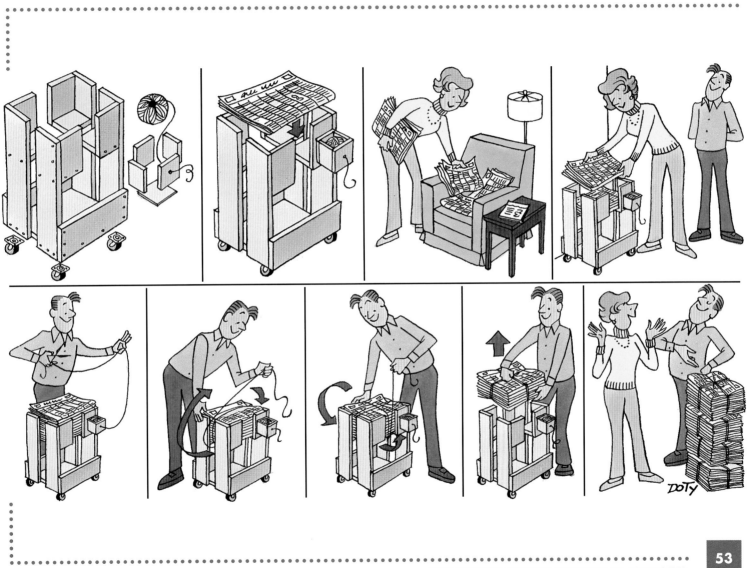

OUR THANKS TO ED FULLWOOD OF MADISON, WI, FOR THIS IDEA.

CAUTION: DO NOT USE PRESSURE-TREATED WOOD

OUR THANKS TO RAYMOND AND SUSAN DAVIS OF RIFLE, CO, FOR THIS IDEA.

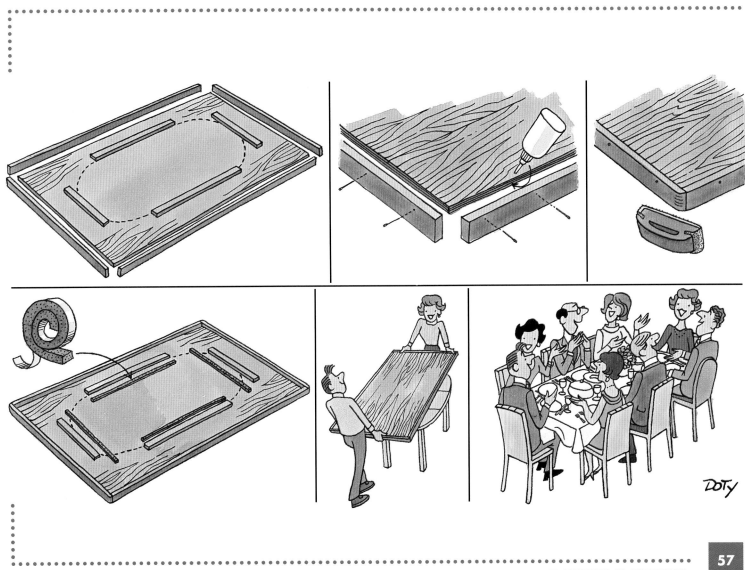

OUR THANKS TO L. M. FRITZ, SOUTHFIELD, MI, FOR THIS IDEA.

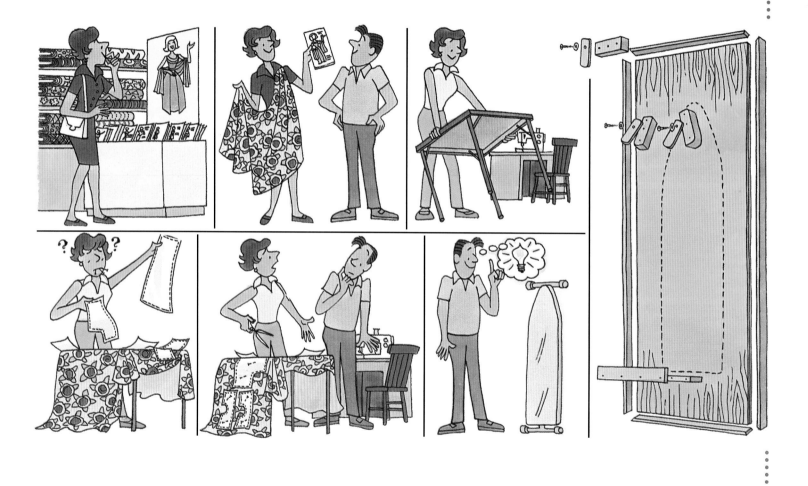

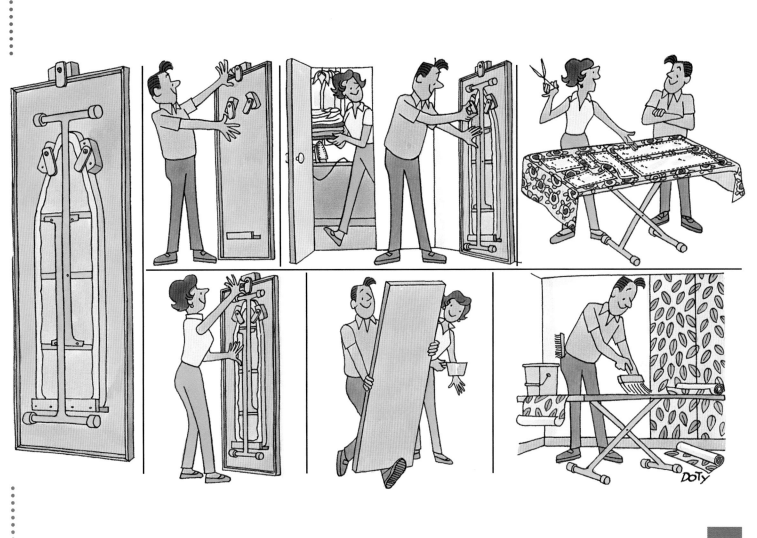

OUR THANKS TO FRED AND JOAN ZAJECHOWSKI OF GRANBY, MA, FOR THIS IDEA.

OUR THANKS TO DON HAMELSTER OF EYOTA, MN, FOR THIS IDEA.

OUR THANKS TO JAMES HORN OF DES MOINES, IA, FOR THIS IDEA.

OUR THANKS TO VIRDALE TOLBERT OF PLEASANTVILLE, NJ, FOR THIS IDEA.

OUR THANKS TO MR. AND MRS. C. M. KINNARD OF EULESS, TX, FOR THIS IDEA.

OUR THANKS TO JEAN DORN, MIAMI SPRINGS, FL, FOR THIS IDEA.

THE
WORKSHOP

OUR THANKS TO DOROTHY BAUMGARTNER OF COLUMBIA, MO, FOR THIS IDEA.

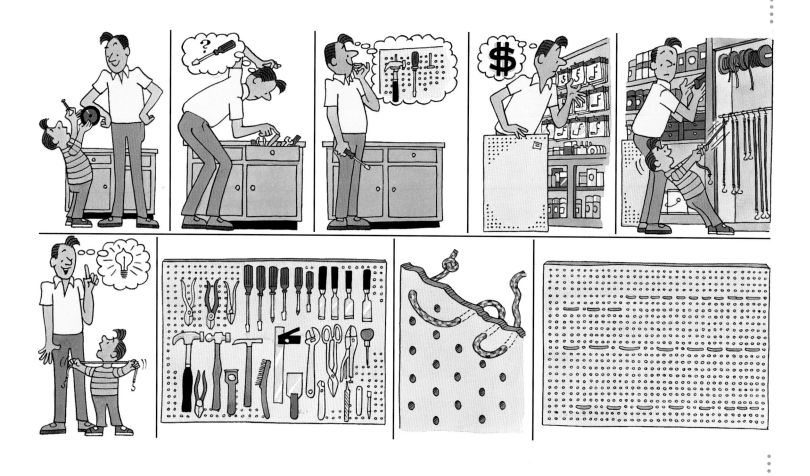

OUR THANKS TO CURT WERLINE OF MADISON, AL, FOR THIS IDEA.

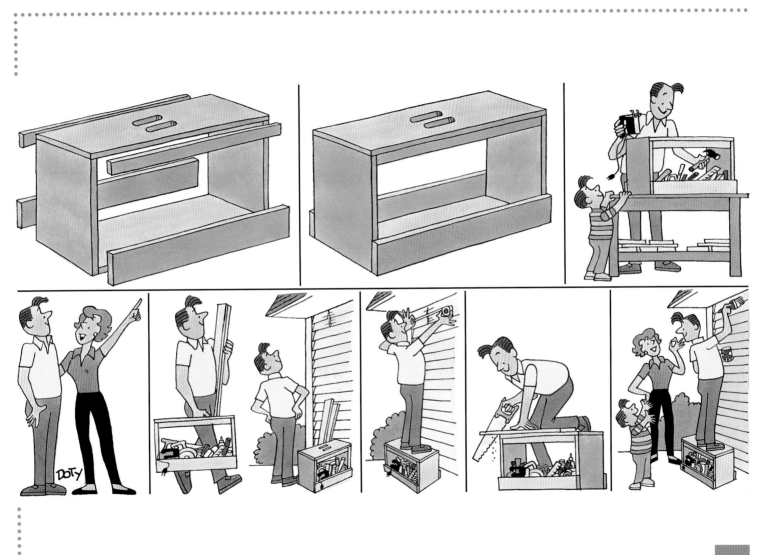

OUR THANKS TO MICHAEL W. MITCHELL OF DANVILLE, VA, FOR THIS IDEA.

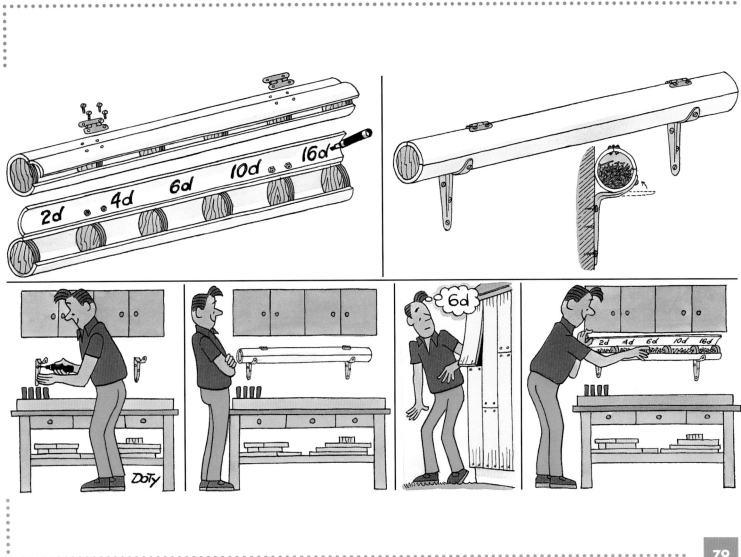

OUR THANKS TO JAMES KELLEY OF HUNTINGDON, TN, FOR THIS IDEA.

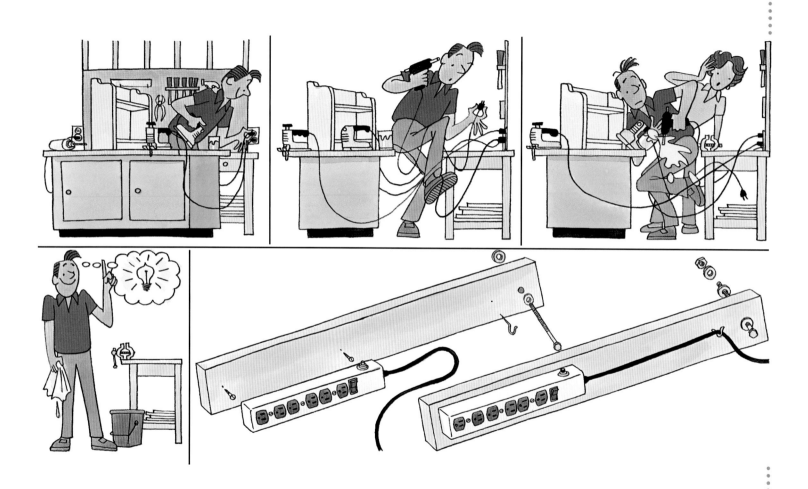

OUR THANKS TO GARY WEINKAUF, EAU CLAIRE, WI, FOR THIS IDEA.

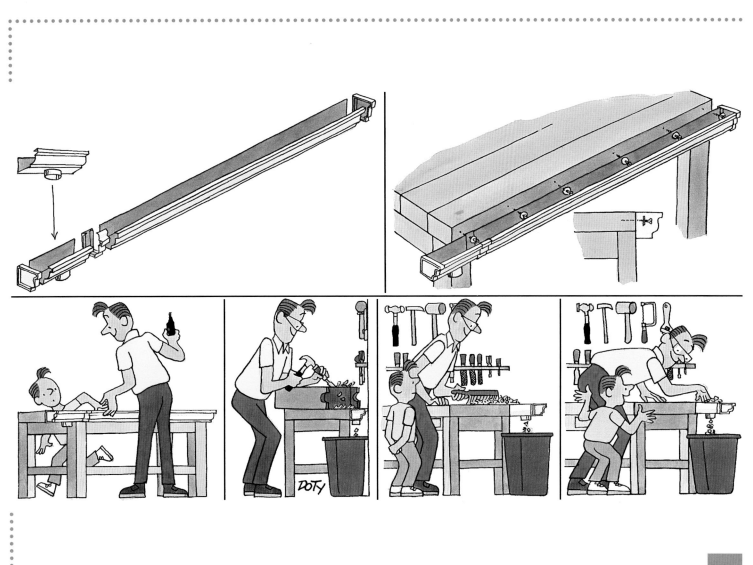

OUR THANKS TO TOM AND RUTH HAULARD OF LATHROP, MO, FOR THIS IDEA.

SPORTS,
TOYS, AND ENTERTAINMENT

OUR THANKS TO RICK TAYLOR OF COON RAPIDS, MN, FOR THIS IDEA.

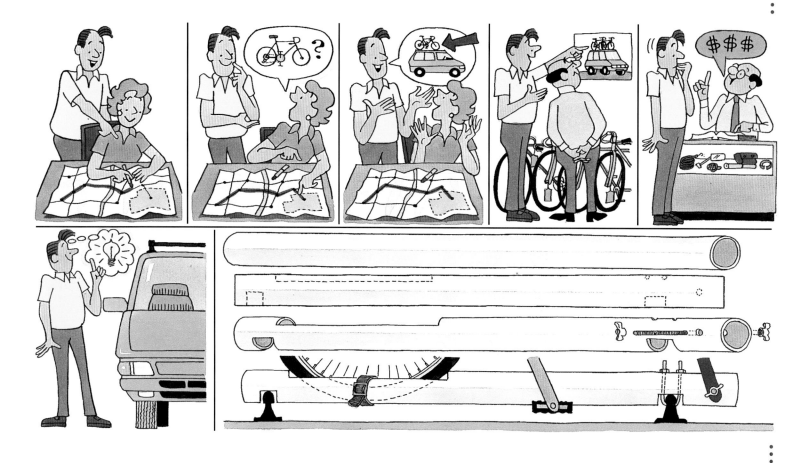

OUR THANKS TO PAUL CHRISTIAN OF APPLE VALLEY, MN, FOR THIS IDEA.

OUR THANKS TO THOMAS MORROW OF WARREN, OH, FOR THIS IDEA.

BAT, BALL, AND GLOVE ORGANIZER

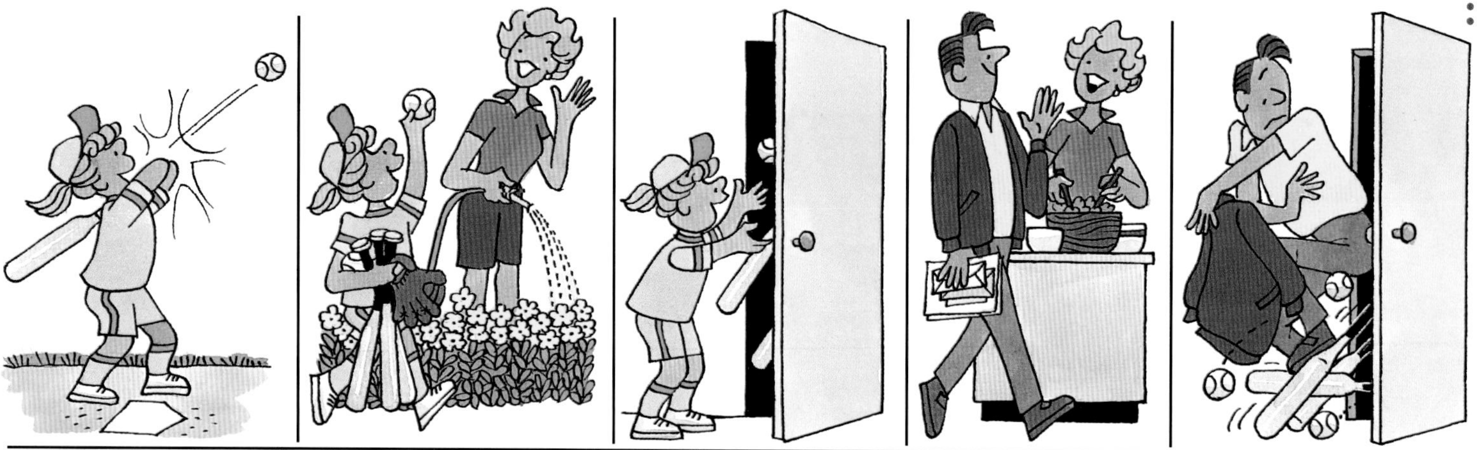

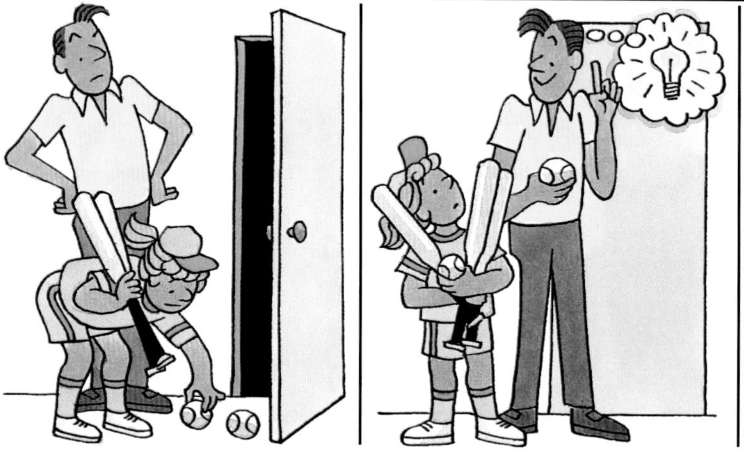

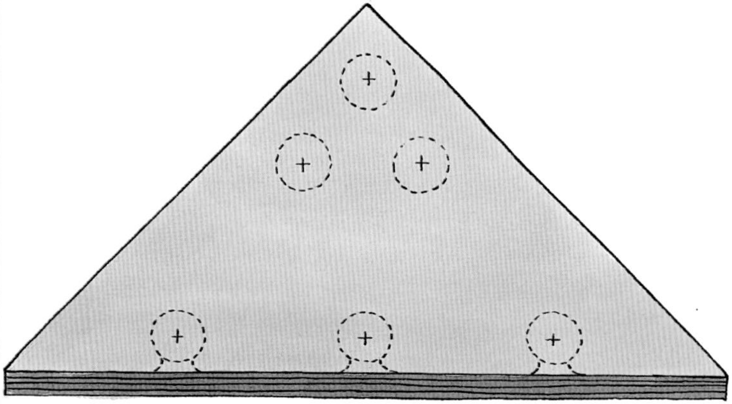

OUR THANKS TO FRED A. RACE OF EUCLID, OH, FOR THIS IDEA.

OUR THANKS TO PHIL LUHN OF SPRINGFIELD, IL, FOR THIS IDEA.

OUR THANKS TO WILLIAM R. SIMONS OF VIRGINIA BEACH, VA, FOR THIS IDEA.

OUR THANKS TO NANCY JOHNSON OF NORTHFIELD, MN, FOR THIS IDEA.

OUR THANKS TO LINDA PARKER OF STEPHENS, AR, FOR THIS IDEA.

OUR THANKS TO STEVE MICHAELS OF ST. LOUIS, MO, FOR THIS IDEA.

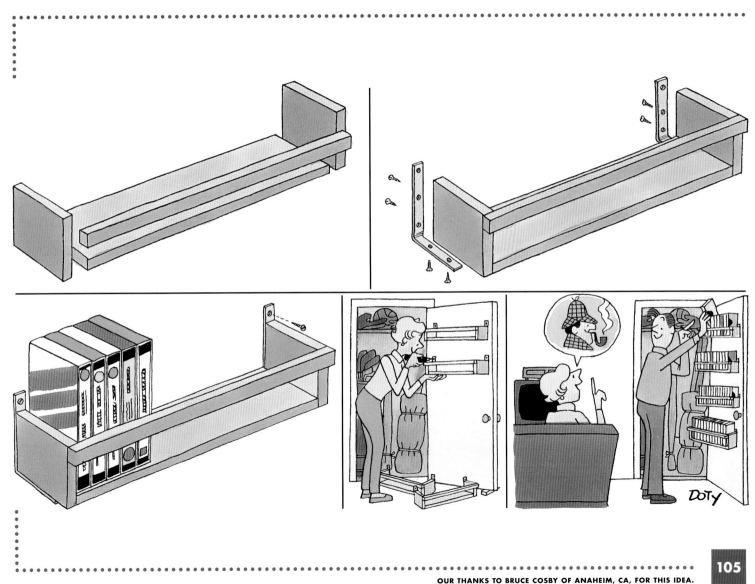

OUR THANKS TO BRUCE COSBY OF ANAHEIM, CA, FOR THIS IDEA.

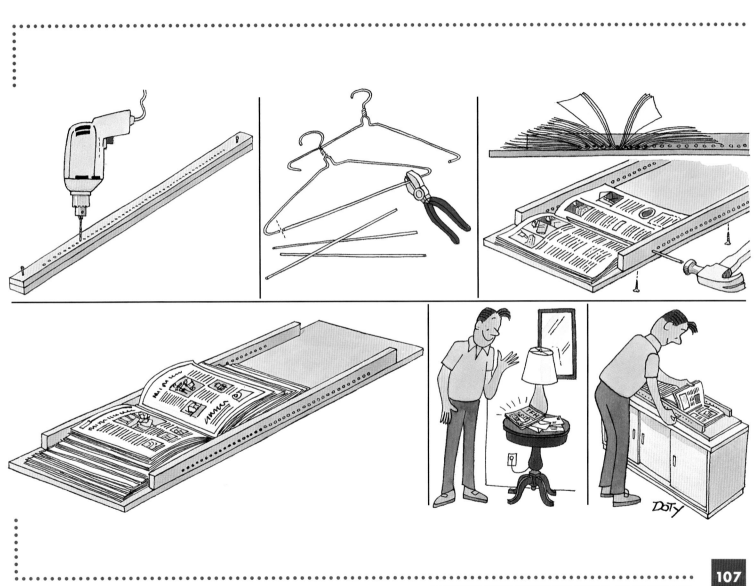

OUR THANKS TO TIM COPELAND OF OAKDALE, MN, FOR THIS IDEA.

THE GREAT
OUTDOORS

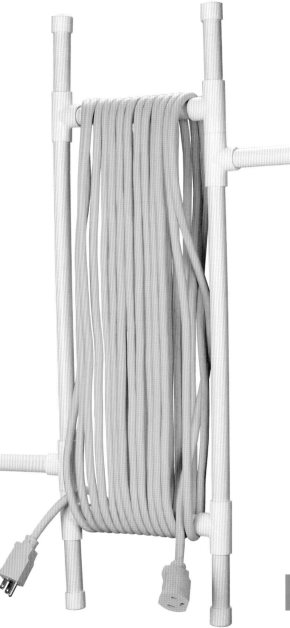

OUR THANKS TO MIKE BROWN OF KALAMAZOO, MI, FOR THIS IDEA.

OUR THANKS TO JIM TRUSHELL OF HOWELL, NJ, FOR THIS IDEA.

OUR THANKS TO LARRY HOLDEN OF TORONTO, ONTARIO, FOR THIS IDEA.

OUR THANKS TO JEFF AND MARY CARLSON OF VERNON, CT, FOR THIS IDEA.

OUR THANKS TO BARNETT HOWARD OF SISTERS, OR, FOR THIS IDEA.

OUR THANKS TO DAVID NUNWEILER OF KANATA, ONTARIO, FOR THIS IDEA.

OUR THANKS TO MICHAEL AND BARBARA BEIN OF AURORA, IL, FOR THIS IDEA.

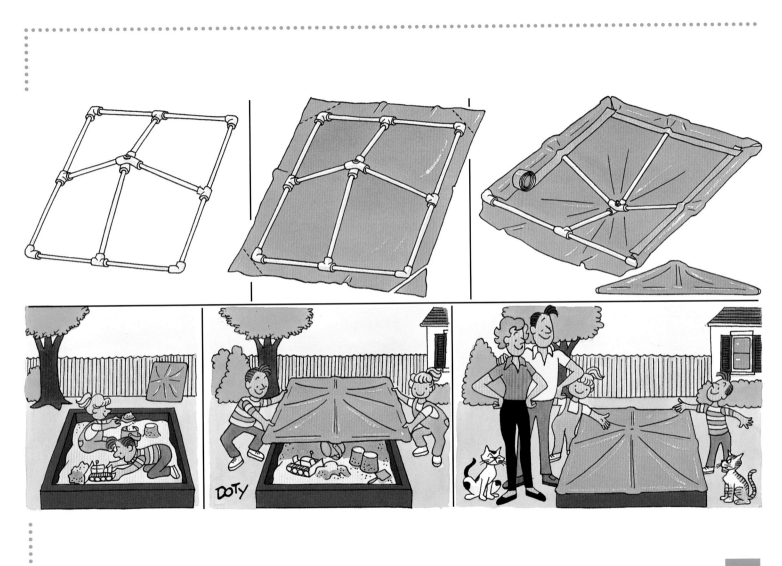

OUR THANKS TO ANTHONY J. NUNEZ OF GREAT FALLS, MT, FOR THIS IDEA.

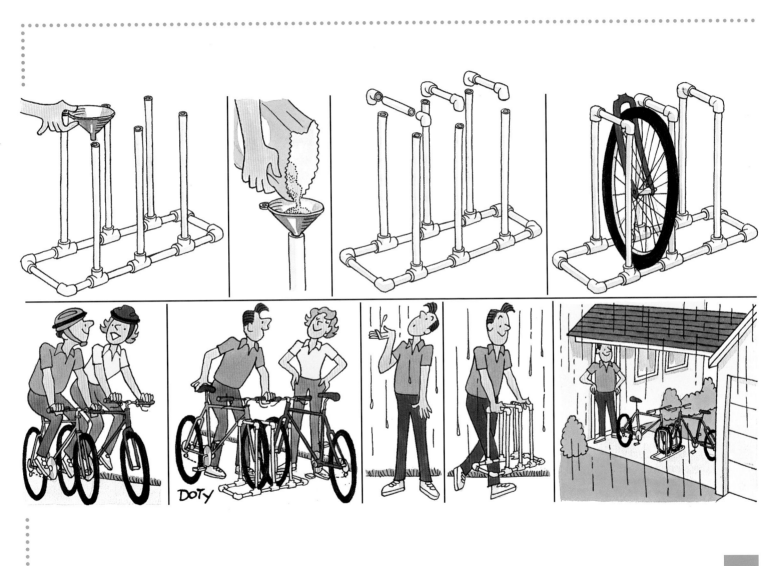

OUR THANKS TO STEVEN M. CONDON OF GOLDEN, CO, FOR THIS IDEA.

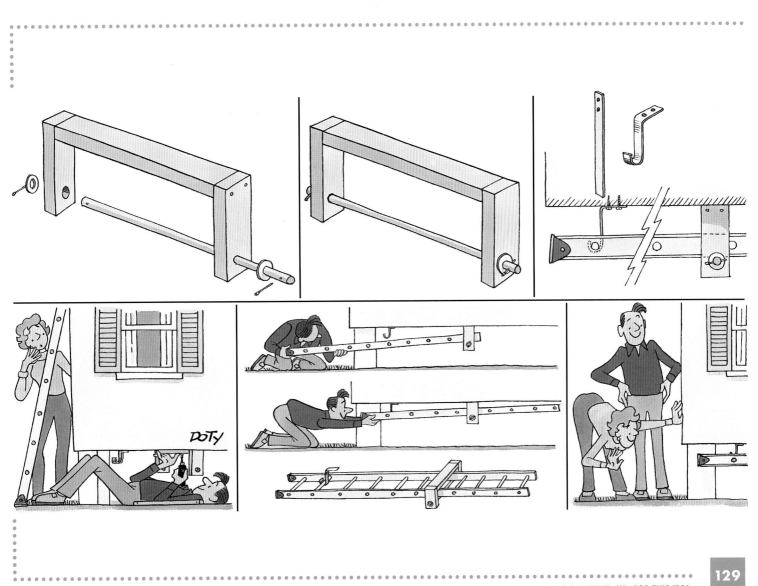

OUR THANKS TO MIKE OTTO OF LAVALE, MD, FOR THIS IDEA.

OUR THANKS TO JOHN ERICSON OF REXFORD, NY, FOR THIS IDEA.

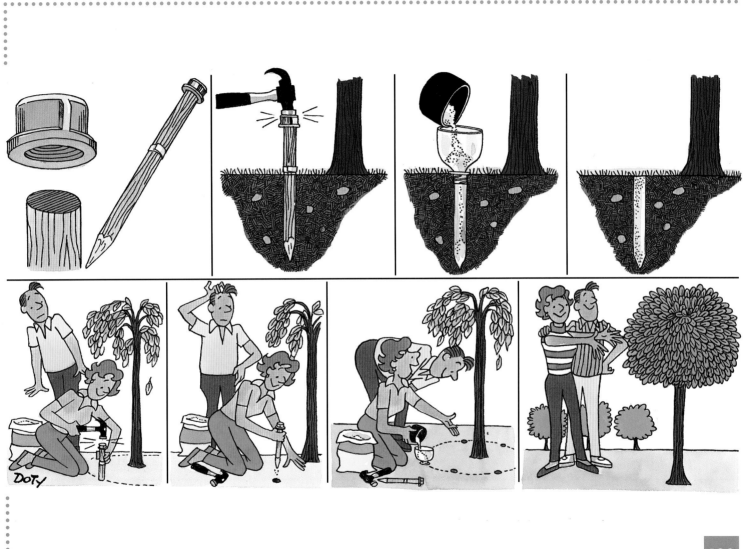

OUR THANKS TO RON POMERLEAU OF READING, MA, FOR THIS IDEA.

OUR THANKS TO WILLIAM FAZER OF POWERS, MI, FOR THIS IDEA.

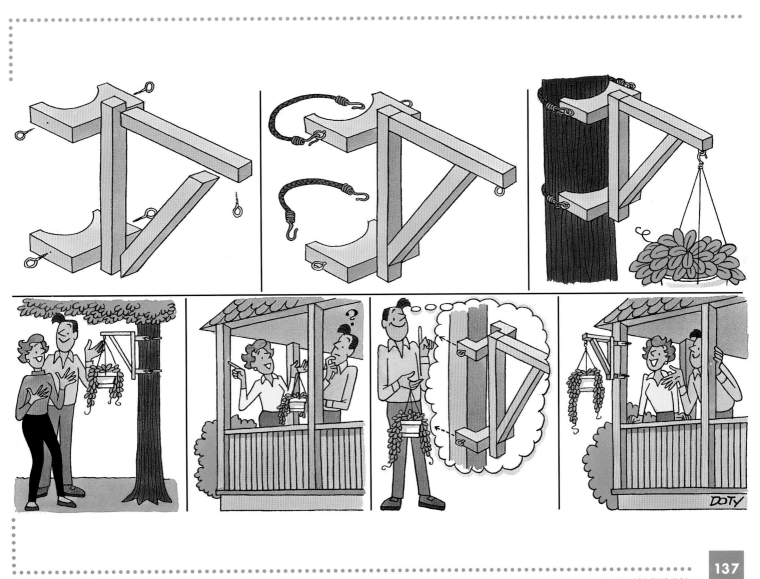

OUR THANKS TO H. BUCK BROWN OF HOLT, FL, FOR THIS IDEA.

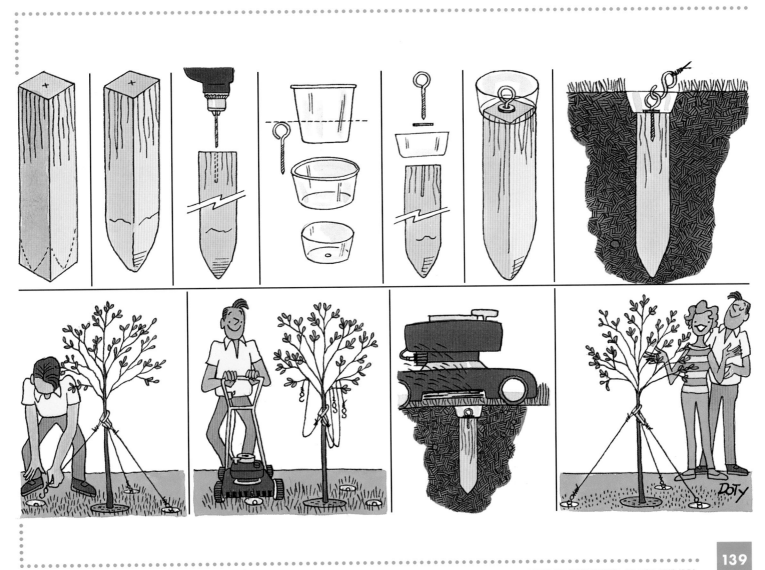

OUR THANKS TO PETER E. DOOMS OF GREENWOOD, IN, FOR THIS IDEA.

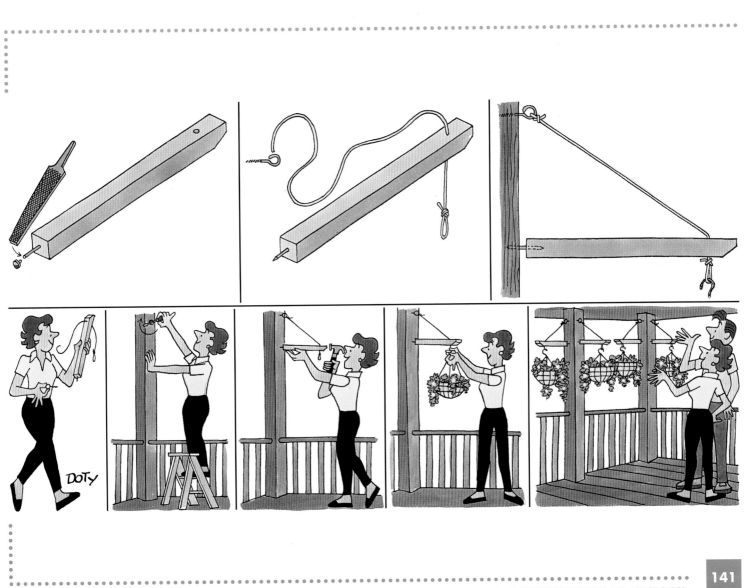

OUR THANKS TO GENE MAYHALL OF DURHAM, NC, FOR THIS IDEA.

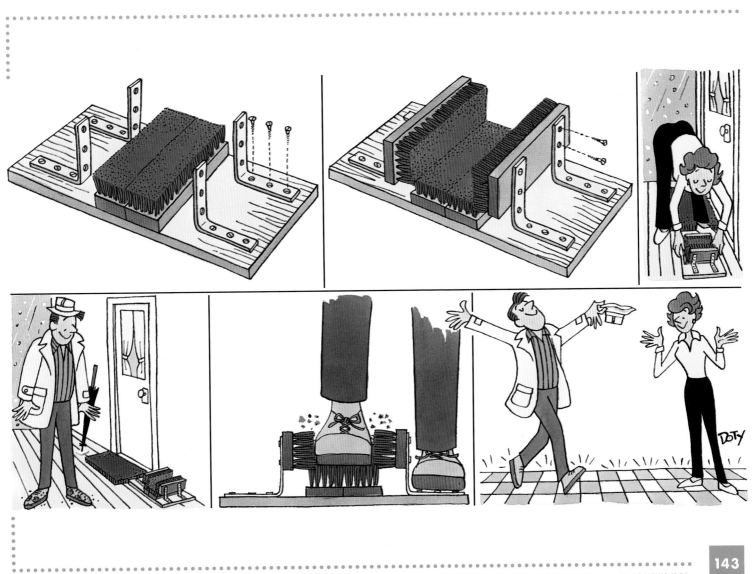

OUR THANKS TO ETHAN HUGO OF HAMDEN, CT, FOR THIS IDEA.

ISBN 0-89577-875-0